MW00791018

HOW TO FALL
IN LOVE WITH
YOURSELF

HELEN HAMILTON

BALBOA.PRESS

A DIVISION OF HAY HOUSE

Balboa Press books may be ordered through booksellers or by contacting:

Balboa Press
A Division of Hay House
1663 Liberty Drive
Bloomington, IN 47403
www.balboapress.co.uk
UK TFN: 0800 0148647 (Toll Free inside the UK)
UK Local: 02036 956325 (+44 20 3695 6325 from outside the UK)

Print information available on the last page.

ISBN: 978-1-9822-8358-2 (sc)
ISBN: 978-1-9822-8359-9 (e)

Balboa Press rev. date: 05/28/2021

TABLE OF CONTENTS

This book is dedicated to all humanity in the hope that it helps us come to love and accept ourselves as we are right now. Only once we may love without limits, expectations and demands upon ourselves will we begin to live and love in our highest potential.

May you fall deeply back in love with yourself and may all internal conflict cease. Let there be peace in your heart.

INTRODUCTION

This book arose out of a clear calling from students who expressed a deep wish to be able to love without limits and without any boundaries. Over and over again it was seen that there was a deep desire in each of us to return to the natural state of Love that we really are, and yet time and time again I saw most of us don't know how to stop judging ourselves and begin to allow the emergence of love.

This book is offered then in the wish that it serves as a gateway to allow the love that is already inside each one of us but perhaps, we don't know how to allow. As you read the chapters that follow and apply them, a deepening sense of acceptance, love and compassion for your own self and others will begin to emerge. Soon you will forget how to judge yourself harshly or negate any part of your existence. Your very Presence will inspire the same in others around you.

It is not our fault that we perhaps don't know how to love our self as yet and we must stop blaming ourselves. Simply through coming to understand what love is and how it moves in our life we will begin to become that love and move away from judging ourselves and others.

First, we will take a look at what love is and perhaps more importantly, what it is not. Second, we will take a look at the stages of love we will move through in our journey. We all start with *conditional love* before allowing *unconditional love* to blossom. We can then move even further to an awakening to the truest non-dual love of the real Self/Reality. Each of these stages will be described and explained so that we may let go of more limited forms of love and move to freer expressions of self-love. Limited is not wrong or bad…it is simply limited.

Lastly, we will look at how we can love our separate sense of self, or ego, into dissolution. As our capacity for love deepens, we can stop rejecting any part of ourselves and begin to live as that highest expression of love in which there is no object of love, but only love itself.

One human being living as this highest expression of love can change the world and inspire many others to do the same. Isn't it time you lived your highest and best life?

CHAPTER 1

What is Love Anyway?

We are here to learn how to love ourselves and the first step is to realise that it is not our fault if we don't already know how to do that. We may have been taught that love is to want to improve ourselves or be better than we are. Whilst this is a noble intention, it will also set us up on a never-ending path of trying to improve what is already here and perfect in this moment. None of us start out feeling our own perfection and in fact, we may be highly skilled at noticing our imperfections. To begin to love ourselves we must come to admit that maybe we don't really know how to do that and that it is not our fault if we don't.

What if we look at our life as an opportunity to learn how to love rather than a place to prove to ourselves that we are no good at it? If you want to learn to drive a car but you have not yet met anyone that can show you how, would you be berating yourself that you cannot drive before having even a single lesson? No, of course you wouldn't, yet each one of us is punishing ourselves deep down inside because we feel we should know how to love our own self and others.

Let's just be honest and say perhaps we don't know how and that we aren't supposed to know how. Can we move around in our life from this orientation? Can we begin to be students of love and lovingness and want to find out what that is? Can we let go of judging, hating and blaming ourselves that we don't seem to know how to love our self? Yes we can! I would urge you to let go of your ideas about love and instead insist on finding out what that really is. We may have seen many examples of loving beings that seem to radiate that love to all and we may somehow be trying to measure up to that standard. What we fail to realise is that the great love for all of humanity emerging from these beings has been allowed, recognised and learned rather than intuitively known. Perhaps it's wiser to say a lot of both has occurred. Sages, Avatars and Teachers of Truth and Love have had to do this exact same opening up and admittance of "I don't know what love is nor how to get it or be it" too. We all start from the same honest place of truth. Love is to begin to admit the truth that "maybe I don't know how to love myself and maybe I am not supposed to know already".

Can the capacity for love be viewed as an art, science or emerging skill? Yes, indeed it can. All of us have been taught to love conditionally and that is where we *all* start. Even the great Sages started from their ideas about what love is and how to do it or be it. We can finally begin to love ourselves more in this moment by accepting that we can love what love actually is, rather than loving our ideas and preconceptions about it. Perhaps even this simple thing is how we be love itself already. Perhaps in admitting we don't know what love is (and have been following what we think it is) is how to love ourselves more.

What happens when we throw out all ideas that we should already know how to be love, to give or receive love or how to love others more? We will immediately be starting from the truest place of all by knowing that we don't know how and that is totally ok right now. Love yourself enough to admit right now with me that you don't know. I don't know how to love either because I don't know what love is. I am in a constant and never-ending unfolding and discovery of what love is. Each and every moment love is revealing another face of itself to me and I LOVE that I don't know what it is. It was a huge relief to admit I didn't actually know nor was I supposed to. Try that on for size and see if it feels good!

CHAPTER 2

The Joy of Loving Acceptance

Once we have realised that we may not know what love is, then it would serve us to spend some time looking at how love acts and expresses itself. This will help us to be clearer on where we are not loving ourselves as yet. Once we can see what love would do in any situation, we can begin to choose that option for ourselves in any moment.

The very basis of love is to **accept what is** and to **accept how we actually are right now**. We are all living with the effects of a very damaging idea that is simply not true and to learn to love we must accept this idea is not true. Here is the idea:

> *"By rejecting what is here in this moment I can change how it is. Rejecting how I am right now will allow me to change and be better".*

This belief is simply untrue. It is not possible to change how the world is, how you are and how all of this is in this moment. I will say this again because it is so important.

***It is not possible to change how
we are in this moment!***

Trying to change how your body and mind is in this moment is the antithesis of love and it is also not going to work! What has already manifested in this moment has *already* manifested. Trying to change what has already shown up as and for us is like trying to sculpt the clay after it has already been shaped, baked and glazed. We must begin to understand that rejecting how things are in this moment is never going to work as a method to make things better. Of course each one of us would like something better than we have in this moment and of course we may want to feel better than we do in this moment but that cannot occur whilst we are rejecting how we are in this moment already. Self-acceptance begins with an honest acceptance of how we are in this moment. If we are angry, then we are feeling angry. If we are feeling happy then we can feel happy as much as possible. If we are judging someone or something in this moment then we can accept that is what is happening without any further blaming of our self.

Wisdom comes when we begin to see that only by totally accepting how our body and mind is _right now_ can we have a chance of something better manifesting in the next moment. All of us waste an amazing amount of time and energy trying to reject what has already manifested in this moment by believing in thoughts that say "should" or "shouldn't". We can allow love to emerge in our experience if we can see the idea that we should be different than we are right now has no basis in reality at all.

It is *not at all possible to change* how you are in this moment!

It is *always possible to accept* how you actually are in this moment AND prefer to be different in the next moment.

<u>Acceptance</u> of what is already here is going to allow things to change moving forward. When we accept how we are right now in the moment, we are for the first time able to start from the right place.

Imagine for a moment asking your GPS to tell you the route to your destination without giving it your starting location. If you set out to be more loving or compassionate towards others, for example, how will you know how to get there if you don't know where you are starting from? Does it make any sense at all to plan a journey without knowing where you are starting from? Where you are is where you are and nothing can change that. How you are right now is how you are and nothing can change that. Coming to accept this can allow us to stop wasting massive amounts of energy rejecting who and what we are in this moment.

If your body and mind are acting in ways you would prefer to let go of, we must accept how it is right now to fulfil this desire.

Acceptance of what already is does not mean liking, condoning, preferring or choosing. It simply means accepting and noticing. It means not being in denial of this moment or at war with yourself.

The perfect stance then is to accept what and who you are in this moment exactly as it is; whilst having an idea of how you would like that to evolve or change in future moments.

So if you are feeling some emotion that you would prefer not to have, that is understandable. But we must come to recognise that it can never leave us if we will not even admit it is here. Each negative emotion, judging thought, self-blaming attitude and sense of unworthiness is also just looking for acceptance from us. They are also just wanting to exist as they are in this moment. Acceptance then becomes a doorway to being able to allow these emotions, thoughts and patterns of behaviour to transmute back into peace.

"Should" and "shouldn't" are based on the idea that we can be different than we are in each moment. If I am expressing anger towards another being, I may feel ashamed of that because I feel I should be able to be more loving in this moment. The truth is that we cannot ever be different to how we are in this moment and peace comes with realising this. This does not mean, however, that we are helpless to stay with the same old unloving patterns for all time. Our mind may assume that acceptance of something may mean that we are stuck with it forever but it is, in fact, exactly the opposite. Only by fully accepting some part of ourselves that we would like to change, can it ever actually change. Agreeing with our mind that we should be different than we are in this moment is absolute self-rejection. It is stating in our energy that "I should not exist as I am right now" and this is why it hurts so much to judge, blame and "should" or "shouldn't" ourselves in any moment. This is self-negation and is the only thing the real Self or Love cannot do.

Love cannot reject anything or anyone yet it also does not make us a "doormat". Loving ourselves more will also allow us to love others more by accepting them as they actually are (rather than what we think they should be in this moment). Therefore, we will be that open space for them in which transformation may happen if it is time for them to change.

I would suggest looking at what emotions, thoughts, actions and patterns of behaviour still occur that you would rather let go of and notice if you are "should-ing" yourself in these moments. Peace develops naturally in our experience when we can distinguish between acceptance and condoning/ allowing/liking etc. Start from where you actually are and see what happens when you do. You may just find qualities emerging from yourself that you have longed for and other things fading away without even trying. It is the nature of the Self that it will always be upgrading itself in manifestation and that will allow for an ever higher expression of who and what you are in each moment. We will begin to experience this as we stop constantly fighting how it already is in some futile quest to get rid of some part of ourselves.

As we begin to be honest about how we are in each moment, then we can accept that these patterns of thoughts, emotions and behaviours are symptoms of our *idea* that we are a separate being, alone and finite in the world. All of our thought patterns have been based on this false assumption and all suffering comes from this. We are not separate from anything at all in reality and we must come to understand that all of our thoughts and emotions have come from this illusionary idea. It is easier to accept those patterns of thoughts, emotions and actions that arise from this false idea of what we are when we see that when we are living in that illusion it feels totally real. When it is experienced as real that we are alone and separate from what we want and need, then it makes sense that we would try to get what we want to make us feel safe and accepted or loved.

Just because we are coming out of that illusionary idea of what we are does not mean we should reject or judge those old ideas about ourselves, others and life as wrong or bad. If we label them this way then we are going to keep playing them out as we keep trying to reject what is here right now. Instead, it can serve us better to simply see our old beliefs and patterns of action as irrelevant, old information based on the assumption of who we thought we were. Rather than rejecting them as wrong and wishing they would go away, *we can begin to love and accept them as symptoms of an old way of thinking.* We can love them by accepting they may still be here but not acting upon them, and we will feel empowered to make higher choices in each moment. If your computer got a software virus you would not blame the computer for not working smoothly, yet we are blaming ourselves for the fact we have not yet found love, peace and acceptance when we are trying to find it from completely the wrong idea about ourselves!

We can simply upgrade our self-definition to seeing what we really are and make an empowered choice to love and accept these old patterns when they present themselves rather than judging or blaming. The very moment we decide to do this, we will begin to feel more peace, love and contentment that deepens into joy over time.

The way to get what you want is to <u>accept</u> what you don't want! Acceptance is a form of love. It is a recognition of Reality as it is in this moment. It is the clear seeing of how you are in this moment.

CHAPTER 3

Understanding Conditional Love

When we first learn to love as human beings, it develops into conditional and limited love. It is important to note that conditional love isn't wrong or bad; but merely conditional. We must let go of defining things so absolutely in order to progress, and perhaps prefer terms like higher or lower, limited or unlimited, fuller or more restricted expressions of love rather than good or bad, right or wrong, better or worse. Everyone is always loving themselves and others to the extent of their current capacity and that can never change through judging or blaming. Unconditional love is not better than conditional. Non-dualistic love is not "the goal" but merely where and how love would like to express itself in and as a human being. It may help to think of your life and spiritual journey as an ever unfolding allowing of love, rather than some place to get to. This is immediately and already allowing more self-love, for love with conditions is quite limited. To say "I will be good enough when I am the non-dual expression of love" is not love - it is a bargain with yourself and a denial of the perfection that you already are but perhaps cannot see as yet.

Conditional love can be viewed as a problem, something that is holding us back or that we need to change and I find many beings viewing it this way. Rather than condemning conditional love, we can take a look at why we love conditionally and begin to understand it. Remember, love is wanting to understand and to know something in its entirety rather than judging or labelling. What if our conditional love was not the issue itself but rather a symptom of our world view? Is it really possible to be the non-dual expression of love when we deeply feel separate to everything else in the cosmos? No, it is not! Is it possible to move from conditional to unconditional love and then to non-dual love with this view point? Not so much!

An understanding of what conditional love is will help us to come to see it as a result, symptom or an effect of the belief in separation. When we are deeply convinced that we are a finite human being only and that we are alone in the universe, separate from everything else, we are constantly living with the effects of that belief. We will feel fear and other negative emotions on a regular basis which all come from the idea that we are one body and mind only. We will deeply believe we were born and are going to die at some point and that is the root cause of all fear. That fear is too great and we have to try to suppress it or project it onto objects we think exist "out there" and separate from us.

Feeling unsafe and that our existence could cease at any moment is the unavoidable effect of believing we are a separate and limited being amongst countless others. We all do many things to try to feel better, more secure, loved and appreciated and this is the basis of conditional love. When we love conditionally, we are really saying "I want to feel safer and I will love you if you stay with me and make me feel secure". There may of course be many variations on this theme, such as "I want to feel worthy/loved/approved of/useful" etc, but all of them are coming as a way to try to feel better. Most of us are trying to get other beings to give us what we feel we need to feel safe and happy; whether that be from our romantic, familial or even professional relationships. We may also be trying to feel secure from acquiring money, fame or some other form of recognition through study or academic achievements etc. None of these activities are wrong but we must begin to see that they cannot give us what we want for any length of time because all the other beings in our life are also trying to get these things from us too.

Again, I have to state that conditional love is not wrong but rather can be viewed as limited in its effectiveness at helping us feel better. If our happiness and security are dependent on other beings, we will always be trying to control or change those other beings on a very subtle level to make sure they stay with us. Our happiness and wellbeing will be fragile and easily upset (if we achieve it at all this way) because nobody can stay with us forever, no amount of money or fame can make us feel safe permanently. Often these "solutions" also come with their own issues.

The realisation will come for each of us at some point that this is not a very effective way to ensure that we feel good, safe and loved. We can come to recognise that nobody can give us what they don't seem to have either. Eventually our loving capacity will feel too small when we are placing demands or expectations on other beings and an urge will come to love unconditionally.

CHAPTER 4

Conditional Love of the self

Conditional love is most limiting when we apply it to ourselves. Most people I meet along the spiritual pathway to awakening are quite unconditionally loving of others already and it's only their own self that they love in a very conditional way. Most people that I meet are demanding so much change from themselves in an effort to feel worthy of love, or even awakening. In my own pathway, I even used my failure to wake up to the truth as a reason to conditionally love myself (unknown to myself at the time) and I see many beings doing this to themselves. Over and over I hear people say that "this would not be happening if I was more awake/enlightened" and expecting themselves to be different than they are in this moment.

Many beings view enlightenment as the ultimate "reward" that will come when they are finally worthy enough; but enlightenment is the total acceptance of what is right now. As we discussed in previous chapters, we must come to love what is already and accept it. Most beings along the pathway have immediately decided they are not good enough just because some negative emotion comes up or they momentarily identify with thoughts. We must come to see that we can love and accept ourselves *as we are in this moment* without placing conditions upon our growth. Love accepts all and can reject none. Love is not a reward for achievement but rather the prerequisite for growth. Can you love yourself just as you are right now? Can you accept that you are the same Self whether you are feeling good or bad? What conditions have you placed upon your own self love?

Almost everyone I meet has an imaginary finish line in their head that states, "when I cross this line then I will be the Self and I will be finished, complete and worthy of awakening, love and all good things". In reality we must see the awakened state is already here and loving our mind and body just as it is right now. This is true whether we feel peace, anger, bliss or grief. This is true whether we are totally and effortlessly aware of our real nature or whether we are totally identified with our mind.

Consider a newly planted seedling in our garden. How much would it grow and prosper if we totally ignored it just because it was not as yet a fully grown plant in bloom? If we said it was not yet worthy of being watered, pruned, fed and loved just because it is not yet where we want it to be, would it ever survive? Of course it would not! This may even seem absurd to consider, yet we are all doing this to ourselves and agreeing it is the best way for us to grow and evolve!

Can you take a moment just to begin to accept yourself as you are? Can you not be a "work in progress" or a "do it yourself" project? You are not a "fix it up" challenge at all. There is nothing wrong with you nor has there ever been. To come to allow a fuller expression of love you must be willing to consider the fact that you have never really seen yourself as you actually are.

Have you ever really looked at yourself as you actually are without the mind's filters of "all the things that are wrong with me that I need to change"?

An awakened being sees nothing wrong with you at all. They see you as a beautiful expression of the One Being playing as a human being for a while. Can you begin to see that this is how you are? You can change your shape as a human being, become more loving, compassionate, patient etc, but you are still always the perfect One Being already. You are so perfect that you can even play with the sense of imperfection. Full recognition of this will allow unconditional love and acceptance of yourself, body, ego and life. Of course, this does not mean that an awakened being stops growing and their mind and body are always in an ever-deepening journey and expression of the truth of their being. The major difference is that they see the perfection that is already here AND allow an ever-greater unfolding of that perfection. Can you begin to see yourself this way too? If not, can you be willing at least to see yourself this way?

Helen Hamilton

Just the simple recognition that you may not be actually at all how you see yourself is key. What you think and feel about yourself may not ever have been true! For how can your mind perceive the truth of your real nature and what you already are?

Be willing to open to the truth and see yourself as all the great Beings that have walked this earth already see you. Just because you may have believed for a very long time that you are broken, damaged or for some reason not good enough or deserving of love does not mean it has ever been so!

CHAPTER 5

Unconditional Love

As our spiritual maturity progresses, we begin to realise that trying to get what we want or need from other beings, our career or our pathway is never going to lead to permanent happiness. If happiness is gained in this way it can easily be lost again and it may occur to us that there must be a better way. Unconditional love emerges from us when we begin to see that nobody else can give us what they don't have. We can come to see that nearly all other human beings on this planet are also searching for love, approval, acceptance and security and they also don't know how to get those things except to try to get it from others.

With a deep understanding developing that everyone else is also convinced that they are a separate being, we can come to accept that they too feel cut off from what they want and need. Spiritual growth really begins to occur much more quickly then, because we can stop blaming others for somehow not being able to fulfil our requirements in a relationship. We may begin to recognise that it is not that they will not make us feel safe, loved or accepted but they simply cannot. The idea that we are a separate being is so widely believed by nearly all of humanity that everyone has been living with the results of that belief for so long. Humanity has learned to accept conditional love as the only option...but it is not so.

It's important to remember that unconditional love is not better than conditional love. This is only how our mind would categorise it. We can begin to use the terms "higher" or "lower" or even "unlimited" or "limited" expressions of love as we see these are only stages we go through as Love itself appears as a human being.

Conditional love is not wrong or bad but merely a symptom of a false idea that has infected our mind. When we recognise this, we can begin to love unconditionally and perhaps even love unconditionally where we are still acting from conditional love in our life. Most of us love each other so deeply, but love our own self very conditionally. What if awakening to the Truth of your being was simply an unfolding of love and its deepening in your life? Would unconditional love blame anything at all? What happens when we love our self unconditionally right where we are in our pathway? Peace is the natural outcome of unconditional love for self and others.

As unconditional love blossoms, we will begin to experience much higher relationships because we are finally just able to spend time with someone without quietly, constantly and internally demanding anything from them. Imagine right now what your life would look like if you did not need or want anything from anyone at all.

A deep and profound understanding of why conditional love happens will automatically allow the emergence of unconditional love in yourself and for others.

As we said before, love is acceptance and understanding of what is. Accepting that nobody can pour you love from an empty cup is accepting what is. Nobody can give anything when they themselves are running on empty.

Unconditional love of our self in our own spiritual pathway

As our ability to love unconditionally develops, we will begin to see how conditional love has been slowing down our progress at awakening to our true nature also. If we are demanding that our own awakening is the only proof that we will accept of our worthiness as an individual, then we will never be able to experience a deep and profoundly stable awakening. We are in fact saying with our energy, "I will know I am good enough when I am awakened fully but the fact that I am not awakened fully means I am not good enough." We are stating that we want to wake up fully but are sure we are not yet good enough for that to happen!

Unconditional love would say that in fact, we don't know if it is even true we are not good enough. We would not place any conditions upon our happiness or worthiness

23

living from this place of a fuller expression of love. As love becomes more unlimited and we need no qualifications to love ourselves we will find that we are enough right now in this moment. We will come to see we are always doing the best that we can in any moment.

Seeing ourselves and others from this viewpoint allows the urge for even greater love to emerge. Naturally, judgement of self and others will begin to fall away as we see that everyone is acting from the misconception that they are separate to everything else in the universe and that they will one day cease to exist. That thought is so scary to human beings that we do anything we can to avoid it. All of human behaviour is aimed at distracting ourselves from that very basic fear in whichever way we can. We also do whatever we can to try to feel safer, happier and more secure.

There is no finish line that we can cross as human beings where we can say we are "good enough" or are "awakened fully" now. There is only what is right now and as we deepen in our own seeing of what is true we will come to live and love from a deep knowing that all is this great One being appearing to be human. You will come to know you are That and you are already perfect as you are right now. You will then be able to allow the never-ending unfolding that occurs in the mind and body of this perfection. It can help to recognise that manifestation of the One being is always occurring and is a never-ending unfolding sculpture. If we imagine ourselves ten years from now, we will seem much more loving, awake and evolved than right now but we will also have traits even then that we are gently moving towards. Only if you take a mental picture of where you are now and where you want to be will you feel you are less than perfect.

Right now, in this moment, you are more than adequate. You can know that because you are the One Great Being appearing as you! For the rest of this lifetime you may be evolving in your mind and body but from the already-so knowing that you are the One. This is a different way to view yourself and it will bring great peace.

Unconditional love of the world and society

All of human suffering comes from this one false idea that we are separate beings alone in the universe. We can begin to see that it is pointless to blame someone (or ourselves) for the actions that anyone does from this false idea. Everyone is convinced this idea is true and therefore has no choice but to act from it. When the great Self appears as a human being it can be convinced for a very long time that it is a separate, isolated individual. How can we ever say then that anyone should be better than they are with this idea still in place? How can we ever expect humanity to stop acting in selfish, unloving ways to other beings when the root cause has not been eliminated?

As much as we would all like society in general to act in loving and kind ways to all beings, we cannot expect this to happen without those beings coming to see the truth of who they really are. The idea of being someone alone in time and space causes great fear in all humans, whether they are conscious of it or not. Most of us are not conscious of it as we suppress it, project it or express it rather than allowing it. Again, we can move away from judgement of others who project that fear onto others and express it as anger or hatred and begin to see that they have no other option! To say that they should act differently is to say they have a choice, and the simple fact is that they don't. As much as our mind would like to keep insisting all human beings have a choice, we don't until we see what is real about ourselves. Only then do we have a choice and can come to choose a higher place and a fuller expression of love.

Fear based actions are a basic fact of all existence as a separate being and we can come to realise that as we move away from judgements and blame. Expecting anyone to act from love rather than fear whilst they still feel they are a separate being is like expecting the symptoms of an illness to go away before we have treated the illness itself. We can begin to look at the problems and challenges in the world today as a symptom of this virus like idea in humanity that we are all separate beings. From this place we are finally empowered to begin to radiate real love, and that in itself is the best thing we can do to help. Just as any animal will react to try to protect itself when cornered, we also do the same as human beings. Those behaviours may have become more subtle and sophisticated but it is still this same basic fight or flight mechanism going on that we see all over the world. It is the root cause of all that we would like to change about the world.

It is important to remember that accepting why people sometimes act in hateful, angry or unloving ways does not mean we are condoning or allowing these behaviours as acceptable.

As unconditionally loving beings we would still take whatever actions are necessary to protect our own life and those of others. We will be much more able to take appropriate actions to protect life from this place without blame. Blaming and "should-ing" are only going to disempower us from actually bringing about real change. If a doctor wants to cure an illness, they must really try to find the cause of that illness and then it can finally be treated in the most effective way. If the doctor merely said to the patient that they shouldn't be feeling those symptoms, then no healing can occur at all no matter what our mind insists.

Most of humanity is not yet able to be vibrationally anywhere near meeting an awakened being or hearing the truth that they are not separate to anyone. Most of us are simply caught in the net of egoic beliefs about our life as a separate being and we keep living out these beliefs over and over. It is only when these beliefs begin to become so painful that the urge arises to find out what is true and no human being can be blamed if that urge for freedom from all ideas is not yet arising in them. We must accept that each human being is the great Self already and it is on its own journey as each human being to come back to the truth of its existence. Unconditional love respects each individual's personal journey and also accepts that someone who has woken up to the truth is not better than someone who is still living as a separate being. There is no better or worse, just simply more expression of love as we progress and less restriction on the allowance of that love.

Acceptance is not weakness or condoning but rather finally empowering ourselves to be able to influence others to make a higher choice. After all, if we are still looking at society through the ideas of "should" and "shouldn't" then we are not yet fully understanding that they simply *cannot* yet make the changes in behaviour we are insisting they should. When we finally understand fully that nobody can change until they actually can, then "should" and "shouldn't" will vanish from our vocabulary and our very Presence will become healing to others and inspire them to want to feel the same way we do and to see the world as we do. This is the highest way to view the challenges in the world today and it will empower us to lift other beings into their highest possible place in any moment.

All great change in the world has been inspired by love and not judgement or rejection of what is.

CHAPTER 6

Love Before Duality

In some beings, we will feel a call to deepen our ability to love even more. Sometimes a deep calling to love without division will appear for us, although we may not realise this is what is occurring. The reality is that none of us are separate from each other and each one of us is more like a wave on the ocean surface, not really separate from anything at all. As love deepens there will be an emerging desire to love completely and before any thoughts.

The moment that we begin to question if there is a fuller expression of love, we will begin to experience it. Love does not need any person or object to love. It is only when we perceive through mind that we feel we are loving someone or something. As we begin to understand and experience that we are not many billions of beings but rather the One being appearing as many, then we can see that all love is Self-love. Whenever we love we are loving our own self even if it *appears* we are loving another human being. We can also come to see that whenever we hate, judge or blame someone else we are in effect doing that to ourselves and this is why we feel bad.

The truth is that all actions, thoughts and words never come from a separate being but from the One being when it is confused about itself. As love deepens into love before duality, we will begin to feel the same love for those we will never even meet as we do for our closest loved ones. Can human beings love with such intensity that it doesn't even matter if we ever meet or know the person we love? Absolutely yes! Whilst we may never know someone personally, we can still love them as we know the most important thing of all, which is who and what they really are. In knowing ourselves to be the One being, we come to know what everything and everyone is. We can begin to embrace all of humanity in our love, knowing that they are not really different than our own self. Our human bodies appear to be separate from each other but that's only how it seems from our mind.

Before duality and the sense of one, two, many or billions of beings occurs, there is only the One Self. Even after the sense of duality arises there is only the One Self. The One Self is appearing everywhere as inanimate and animate objects, sentient and insentient forms. The more sentient the form is that it takes, the more it will seem to be able to love but even the single celled amoeba will love its own self and try to preserve its existence. Each and every creature is driven by this urge for self-preservation which is a form of self-love.

Loving without division

How can we begin to love as and from the One? What must change within us to allow this deepening of love? To allow this purest form of love we must be willing to question our most basic assumption of all; we must be willing to ask if there is really anyone else to love! Is there really a world full of beings? Are there any "other" beings or is there simply lots of human bodies appearing inside your own Self? To simply want to find the answer to these questions is already the emergence of non-dual love. To want to experience before the sense of "other" arises is the purest way to perceive reality. Is there really all these other beings and other things? Or could the universe simply be a collection of all the different shapes you are appearing as?

As amazing as this may be to think about, it is what is already true even now. Our own Being is appearing as billions of human bodies and in each one it may be convinced it is separate to everything and everyone else, but the truth is that it is not. When one human being perceives from this place before duality arises, then the power of that love begins to change everything. We can all come to see that each and every being is another way that our own Self is appearing in a never-ending unfolding of unique and individual expressions that are ever more wonderful.

The sense of "other" will still be present even when we are able to love before duality and it will always seem like there are other beings. It is important to know that we can respect the individual way the Self is appearing as and in each person we meet, whilst still recognising their true nature is the same as our very own self. There is only the One Self but it can appear as an infinite number of different expressions. In each human being it will look different, talk and think differently, it will like different foods, have a different sense of humour and be totally unique. Just like each and every wave on the ocean surface is unique but not separate to the ocean, we are all manifestations of the One Self. We must learn to love the essence or source of ourselves in which there is no difference at all.

Everyone we meet from this place before division into "me and other" will be subtly affected by our energy and lack of internal conflict. We will be able to make a positive impact on the world simply by our very existence and example to others. We can only move forward as a species if we are willing to embrace what is the same for all humans, rather than focusing on what makes us different. We can come to see that each human being is us and is deserving of our respect because of that. Everything in existence is the One Self and we can hold it inside our own heart with the reverence of knowing its real Source. This is the only permanent way to heal the challenges we face as human beings today and it starts with each one of us being willing to love before division. Before the sense of "other" even arises, there is nothing outside or separate to you; all of this is you.

CHAPTER 7

Love and Relationships

In this chapter we will look at how we can allow love to express itself in our relationships. As our capacity to love increases, we can come to see there really is no relationship between two beings; but only the One Self playing as these roles. Loving before division allows the Self to experience what it is like to be an individual and unique but without any needs or wants coming into the relationship. Whether the relationship is with a family member, a romantic partner or a professional colleague, we can see the basis of the relationship is to allow the ever-greater expression of love. When we view relationships from this perspective, we can allow an ever-deepening expression of love. The way that love expresses itself will be different based on the nature of the relationship but the challenges in each relationship will be there to allow love to blossom.

Respect, appreciation, gratitude, admiration, loyalty and trust are just a few of the ways that love will express itself and it helps us to know that love is always looking for a deeper expression. When we orient our lives and relationships from that viewpoint, we can see that any potential issues must be a calling for the relationship to deepen. Let's take the example of a romantic relationship or marriage between two beings when a decision has to be made on how to do something. Both people in the relationship have different opinions on what the outcome should be. When we see from the egoic or separate sense of self and we believe in "other" than us we will only see two solutions; we will see a solution in which one or the other wins and the decision goes their way. Our egoic sense of self can only think in terms of "either/or" so it will feel as though either "I win" or "I lose" in a situation like this. When we love before duality and division, we can see that these two opinions are really from the same One being and we can hold a space for a third solution to appear in which both original opinions are included. Even if only one partner in the relationship is able to love before duality this third option can still present itself.

In this way a relationship becomes a place where many minor miracles and wonderful things can manifest as love blossoms. Each opinion goes into the melting pot and something even better than either of them becomes an option, where it wasn't before.

Relationships are a mirror of our own self

When we know that there is only the One Self we can allow our relationships to be a place of conscious loving growth and respect. Each being that we are in relationship with will show us some aspect of ourselves that perhaps we haven't fully embraced as yet. If we can recognise that how another being treats us or makes us feel is a reflection or mirror of some unresolved feelings inside our own self, then we are empowered to heal ourselves and the relationship at the same time.

If, for example, another being is seeming to judge us quite harshly then we can see that we must be judging our self deep down. Looking for where we are not accepting how things actually are (as we learned in the previous chapters) will allow the relationship to change. The other being IS our self and so can only reflect back to us what we feel deep down. The moment we begin to love and accept our own self more, then the relationship must come to mirror that back. We don't know how that will manifest of course, and it is important to remember that sometimes this means the two beings in the relationship will grow closer and sometimes they may feel called to move apart. What we can know is that however the healing occurs in the relationship, it will mean more love, acceptance and respect for both the people involved.

Sometimes we may notice that some or all of our relationships are functioning from a place of conditional love in which both beings want or need something from each other. As our loving expression grows, we may feel this to be too confining and each relationship will go through a transformation and healing. If we can remember that each healing is an allowance of greater love to blossom then we can work through these transformations much easier. Our relationships then become an exploration of what it is like to be in that relationship without needing or wanting anything at all from each other. We can discover that there is no end point for the capacity of love to increase and there is nothing more joyous for human beings than to consciously allow love to blossom without any limits. Relationships that we create from this expression of non-dual love will tend to be freer, lighter and more fun whilst serving each being involved and facilitating ever greater growth and self-expression. It is wonderful to be able to consciously grow together with someone and see how far love can stretch itself in this lifetime.

CHAPTER 8

Loving Our Ego Into Dissolution

Perhaps the most challenging aspect in loving ourselves more occurs once we are on a pathway to awakening. We may have had a few glimpses of our real Self and the peace and clarity that comes with it, or we may have simply had enough of suffering. For all of us at some point, some egoic patterns come to the surface and some old ways of thinking return. We may experience periods of peace, but then perhaps fear, guilt or anger seem to return or maybe we keep living out the same old tired experiences in our lives.

We can see that love would perhaps embrace what arises in ego but how to actually do that in practice? Can we apply what we have learned so far to this situation? Let's look at this and try to understand why we find it so challenging to embrace these patterns when they arise.

Remember that we said love is understanding? Well, now it is more important than ever. We can begin to look at our egoic sense of self as a bunch of thoughts, emotions and experiences that are symptoms of the former idea that we had about ourselves. When we begin to understand why we used to think and feel this way, then we will be less able to reject whatever arises in each moment. The basic fact is that when we believe we are a separate being we feel compelled to try to get what we think we want and need from life, from God or from other beings. We have not known any other way and we must understand this. To reject these patterns of behaviour is going to put us back in conditional love for our self and in ego. Instead, we can recognise that we had no other choice but to think and feel as if we really were separate to everything else. These ways of thinking may now have been seen to be untrue, but we must remember that just because we now prefer to be more loving, compassionate and we value what is true, it does not mean that somehow our brains begin to automatically think in ways of truth. Each one of us has a human mind that still thinks in ways of separation and conditional love. When we understand this is not going to change by rejecting it then we have a chance to transcend these patterns by loving them.

In the moments when ego arises and some old thought pattern occurs, or we say something unkind or get angry, we can be tempted to judge ourselves. It is vital to remember that we can accept what has shown up for us already in this moment AND have a wish to live more from the Truth of our being. We can begin to welcome and accept these egoic patterns when they arise if we see they are coming back up because we are asking to live from and as the Truth.

Only once these patterns arise can we make a choice to live from the Truth of our being, to live before duality and division. We must make that choice when these old thoughts arise and see that we are being given a chance to see that these thoughts, emotions, beliefs and actions are simply not relevant to the real Self.

We must begin to notice these thoughts are not true for the One Being **but also not make them wrong or bad**. Nearly everyone I meet on the pathway is rejecting their old way of thinking as "bad" or "wrong". This is not love before duality but actually conditional love. What we are saying in effect is, "I am loveable only if I never revert back to egoic patterns".

Each time an old pattern arises, we can see this is another chance to recognise that it simply no longer applies to us from what we have seen in our journey to Truth. We can begin to look at these old patterns as just "old software" and we are now getting an upgrade. When you get a newer car, phone or laptop, you don't spend any time at all saying that your old device is wrong, bad or should not exist; you simply let it be and move onto something higher.

We can view our old egoic thinking from this place too. Each time we lovingly welcome some emotion we would rather not be feeling, or question if some old separation thinking is really true, we are being that non-dual love in this moment. We are living it. Each time we reject, deny, push away or say it should not be arising, we are being our egoic sense of self in this moment.

Love wants to embrace and understand rather than choose. Love before division into "me and other" does not see "ego and Self" at all. It just sees older thinking patterns that are not so relevant now. We can simply classify them as more limited or restricted thinking patterns and we can gently allow them whilst preferring our newer, less limited thoughts and experiences of being the Self. This is real love in each moment. This is a total lack of ability to deny or reject, to judge or to push away and it empowers us to move beyond these old ways.

An awakened being has done exactly this; every awakened being has done exactly this. They have simply chosen to include, understand and accept consistently. We can all make this same choice to include and accept and understand. We don't need to automatically go into division when our old ways of being arise because we can come to see these are simply just habits of thinking and feeling and will persist for a while. When we push against our old mindset, we are not allowing these thoughts to leave. We are saying energetically "I should not be how I am in this moment; these thoughts should not be here right now". We are already the One being and anything we state with our energy has to occur. We are saying we need these thoughts and feelings to leave and so they cannot actually leave. We will continue to need them to go and they will not actually be able to. The universe will move to agree with our need. When we come to understand this, we will see we can never be free of egoic patterns by pushing against their presence. We must make a choice to notice them and allow them to be whilst not identifying with them. This is the highest way to love them.

When we simply allow these patterns and let them be without believing them, we are in the perfect expression of love. We are not saying it must be "Self OR ego" but really "Self and ego" and we are undivided. Our egoic patterns will begin to dissolve the very moment we don't allow ourselves to be divided and instead we choose to love. Ego is always pushing against or trying to grab hold of something and it is precisely this very simple movement that sustains our egoic sense of self. When negative thoughts or emotions arise, we can simply notice the urge to push them away and not act upon it. When positive states of love, joy and peace arise we can simply notice the urge to want them to stay and not act upon this either. In this very simple way, we stop being the ego and start being the Self in a real and lived way. This is a very simple, profound and yet practical way to orient our lives.

Whatever mind or ego labels as "bad" will be accompanied by an urge to reject it when it arises. We can see this when fear comes or when we have some very noisy thoughts. We can also notice that whenever something good comes, like bliss, it is always accompanied with an urge to try to get it to stay. What would happen to our life if we simply allowed these two basic urges without identifying with them? Each human being is programmed to move towards pleasure and away from pain, but we don't have to automatically do this. Wisdom dawns for us when we can see these two movements as simply an older way of reacting to whatever arises inside or in our outer world. We can see this was a valid response before from the divided state of consciousness, but is not so relevant now. In this way we will live from and as the Self at all times. Gradually the things we label as "not wanted" will begin to disappear and the things we label as "wanted" will come more often and get ever more amazing.

This is the very simple way to love our ego into dissolution.

CHAPTER 9

The World is Yourself

As we progress in our ability to love, we will feel a call to begin to love the world as we see it and we will begin to recognise we have a chance at influencing real change. The important thing to realise is that there is not actually a separate "you" moving around in the world and interacting with other beings. Everyone that you meet and that will ever exist is your own Self. There is only the One of us here. Once we deeply grasp this, we can see that loving our own self becomes even more important and a catalyst for change on a global scale.

We can also come to see that judging and blaming what happens in the world is only going to hurt our own self because it is the same as judging our self. Anything that we are pushing away or rejecting in the world as wrong or bad is only going to cause us to feel even more divided. Let us remember again here that accepting what is happening in the world and all the things we see on the nightly news is not condoning or agreeing with it but simply accepting where we are as a species right now. The human race is capable of the greatest love of all and it is also capable of the worst atrocities possible. We can accept that these extremes of behaviour are not actually opposites but merely the symptoms of the One being recognising itself everywhere clearly or feeling alone and isolated.

You are everywhere all the time and you are all that ever existed in the past, all that exists right now and will exist in the future. You are appearing as the infinite diversity of shapes and forms and will continue to do so forever. You cannot be absent from anywhere so anything at all you see happening is your own self. We must take responsibility for this as the One being and not as a personal self. To simply blame ourselves for what we see happening "out there" only serves to cause us more suffering and leave us powerless to change anything. Consider how many beings have tried to make the world a better place and failed because they were trying to achieve this as a separate "someone". We can also look at those that left a mark on this planet and who people remember thousands of years after they left their body. These are all great beings who embraced their ability to love beyond all condition and limitation.

Any rejection of anything at all in the world is a self-rejection and will diminish our power to create real change. Any negation of anything at all is a negation of our own self.

The only way to heal the world then comes from our own emerging capacity to love it. Love wants to understand why the atrocities, injustices and acts of discrimination occur and what leads to them rather than simply saying they should not happen. When we learn first how to love our own self without limitation, then we are finally in a position to embrace society exactly as it is with understanding, wisdom and compassion. These energies inspire change in others around us and empower everyone to have a chance at tasting the peace of the undivided Self.

The best way to help the world is to become the teachings in this book and show others that there is a different way to live. The world needs many more examples of empowered beings that have consciously recognised themselves as a unique expression of the One Self. Each one of us that wakes up to the Truth of what we actually are and lives as that is going to lift the whole human race and make higher choices possible for those beings around them. If only one individual did this then we have another Krishna, Buddha or Christ on the planet. If a hundred people did this, we would have a significant change occurring on the planet. If a thousand people fully embraced the teachings in this book then the world would begin to look extremely different. There would be sharing of resources, help available to all that need it and a lack of conflict internally and externally. Satsang would be seen as an essential part of our education as human beings and offered to all who want it. How can we ever be free of wars and violence as a species if we are still at war with our own self? How can we ever act for the wellbeing of all individuals if we still feel our own self to be separate to everything else?

This is your chance to make a real difference in the world. To recognise yourself as that Supreme Love is powerful and any actions you make then become so much more effective as they come from the place before division and duality. Start with your own self and become a loving example of what is possible for any human being.

CHAPTER 10

The Only Choice We Have

Each one of us has a choice in every moment to love conditionally or to love without limits or boundaries. We must decide whether to accept what is or to reject it. Each time we push against ourselves, other beings or the world as it is, we are living as our egoic self. Each time we embrace what is right now whilst wanting more for the next moment we are living as the Undivided One. Such a powerful choice is available to you in every moment now you have understood how to love.

We are all called to begin to love ourselves more and then to allow that love to overflow into our lives, families and other relationships. From there the love will continue to spread outwards from us like a never-ending ripple on the surface of a lake. It all starts with making a choice to love in each moment. Each time we choose to love something or someone exactly as they are, we hold them in a great love that can be transformative for them and us. When we choose to love we can all benefit from it.

Truly, the only choice we have in any moment is whether to love or judge. We can love our own flaws and failures first and forgive ourselves just as we are. As we practice loving ourselves, we can then begin to love others much more easily because we will not need anything from them at all. Imagine your relationships when they are built on mutual love and respect and nothing can damage that. Imagine your capacity to love increasing daily. The more we want to love the more we are able to. Soon you will be able to embrace the whole world in your love.

Wherever you are right now in your desire to be more loving as you read this, start with your own self. You deserve love and you are totally lovable just as you are right now. I don't need to know anything else about you to know you are lovable as you are the One great Self. I know what you are and I know your capacity for love. Just make a start and choose to love in this moment, for this is the only choice we really have or need.

You are loved

If you would like more information about Helen Hamilton, her live Satsangs, silent retreats and classes please contact us:

Our website is www.helenhamilton.org

Find us on Facebook by searching @satsangwithhelenhamilton

Search for us on Youtube at "Satsang With Helen Hamilton"

Email us at evolutionofspirit@gmail.com

.

Made in United States
North Haven, CT
29 August 2024

56687472R00039